Hannah Farley-Hills for HFH Productions
presents

SURRENDER

by Sophie Swithinbank

in creative partnership with Phoebe Ladenburg

Surrender previewed at Tom Thumb Theatre, Margate, in 2023 and was first performed at Arcola Theatre, London, on 19 June 2024

SURRENDER

by Sophie Swithinbank
in creative partnership with Phoebe Ladenburg

Cast
Mother — **Phoebe Ladenburg**
Jean (VO) — **Eleanor Wright**

The approximate running time is 70 minutes.
There will be no interval.

Creative Team
Co-Director — **Sophie Swithinbank**
Co-Director — **Phoebe Ladenburg**
Director Associate — **Nancy Medina**
Lighting Designer — **Stacey Nurse**
Sound Designer — **Dominic Brennan**
Costume Designer — **Pam Tait**
Movement Director — **Jess Tucker Boyd**

Production Team
Stage Manager — **Rose Hockaday**
Press Representative — **Kate Morley PR**
Production Artwork — **Alan Harford**
Production Accountant — **Alan Mackintosh**

Produced by **Hannah Farley-Hills** for HFH Productions

Phoebe Ladenburg | Performer and Co-Director

Phoebe Ladenburg is a multi-award-winning actor, director and theatre maker. Her directing/dramaturgy credits include *Clown Sex* for stage and audio (nominated for two Off West End Awards, Vault Festival People's Choice and winner of an Independent Podcast award), *The Journey* (4*, Pleasance Theatre), *The Bacchanals* (4*, Mikra Theatricals), *Bacon* (Clapham Omnibus, Arcola Theatre, Nick Hern Books), *The Superhero* (Lyric Hammersmith) and *Hot Wheels* (British Youth Music Theatre).

Her acting credits include *Baby Shower* (Turtle Canyon), *Passing* (Bunker Theatre) and *Nine Weeks* (Arts Theatre). Her performance as Linda in *Tuesday* (White Bear, Nick Hern Books) won critical acclaim. She won Best Actress at the 2024 Tokyo International Short Film Festival and was nominated for the Spotlight Prize in 2015.

Sophie Swithinbank | Playwright and Co-Director

Sophie Swithinbank is a multi-award-winning playwright and screenwriter, based in London. She is the 2023 winner of the Peggy Ramsay/Film4 Award. Sophie's play *Bacon* (Tony Craze Award Winner 2018) ran at Finborough Theatre in 2022, to critical acclaim, winning four Off West End Awards. Bacon toured the UK, Melbourne and New York in 2023–24. Sophie is also developing Sexplay with HFH Productions. Sophie was on attachment at the National Theatre 2023-24, developing a new play.

For theatre her credits include: *Beans* (National Theatre Studio), *Even in Arcadia* (longlisted for Verity Bargate Award 2020), *Circle Game* (Southwark Theatre, shortlisted for Phil Fox Award 2020), *Where There Is Smoke* (National Theatre Learning), Come Inside (Bush Theatre) and *The Superhero* (Lyric Hammersmith).

For TV: *BACON* (developed with NBC Universal) and *L/OVER* (MTV Finland).

For film: *Body Broker* (developed with Eleven/No Ordinary).

Nancy Medina | Director Associate

Nancy Medina is Artistic Director of Bristol Old Vic, taking the role in 2023. In Oct 2023 she directed her first production for the theatre, a revival of Tarell Alvin McCraney's *Choir Boy*.

As a director, her credits include *The Darkest Part of the Night* (Kiln Theatre), *Moreno* (Theatre503), *Trouble in Mind* (National Theatre), *The Half God of Rainfall* (Fuel / Birmingham Rep / Kiln Theatre), *The Laramie Project* (Bristol Old Vic Theatre School), *Two Trains Running* (Royal & Derngate / ETT / RTST), *Strange Fruit* (Bush Theatre), *Collective Rage: A Play in 5 Betties* (Royal Welsh College of Music and Drama), *When They Go Low* (NT Connections / Sherman Theatre), *Yellowman* (Young Vic), *Romeo and Juliet*, *As You Like It* (GB Theatre), *Curried Goat and Fish Fingers* (Bristol Old Vic), Dogtag (Theatre West), *Strawberry & Chocolate*, *Dutchman* (Tobacco Factory Theatres) and *Persistence of Memory* (Rondo Theatre).

She is a recipient of the following awards – 2024 Genesis Foundation Prize, 2020/2021 Peter Hall Bursary (National Theatre), 2018 RTST Sir Peter Hall Director Award (Royal & Derngate/English Touring Theatre), 2017 Genesis Future Director Award (Young Vic) and 2014 Emerging Director's Prize (Tobacco Factory Theatres).

She was a visiting director at the Bristol Old Vic Theatre School and was joint Artistic Director and founder of the Bristol School of Acting.

Stacey Nurse | Lighting Designer

Stacey is a multifaceted Theatre Technician, Lighting Designer and Stage Manager.

Recent credits include: *For Black Boys Who Have Considered Suicide When The Hue Gets Too Heavy*: as Assistant Stage Manager (New Diorama, Royal Court, Apollo Theatre Shaftsbury), *To Hold My Love*: as Lighting Designer (The Place, Resolution Festival), *Summer Camp for Broken People*: as Stage Manager and Lighting Designer (Pleasance London and Edinburgh Fringe), *Blueprints*: as Stage Manager and Lighting Designer (Pleasance London and Edinburgh Fringe), *I Love You Now What*: as Stage Manager (Edinburgh Fringe), *Brenda's Got a Baby*: as Stage Manager (New Diorama), *Between the Lines*: as Stage Manager (New Diorama).

Dominic Brennan | Sound Designer

Dominic Brennan is a composer and sound designer from West London. Previous shows include: *The Children* (Nottingham Playhouse), *The Misandrist* (Arcola Theatre), *STRIKE!* (Southwark Playhouse), *Mediocre White Male* (Park Theatre), *Spiderfly* (Theatre 503), *Cuckoo* (Soho Theatre) and *The Universal Machine* (New Diorama Theatre) – a musical co-written with David Byrne (new Artistic Director at the Royal Court Theatre). In 2017 he won the Off-West End Award for Sound Design for his work on *Down & Out in Paris and London* (New Diorama Theatre). Other work includes music for adverts, short films and a sound installation at the Princess of Wales Conservatory in Kew Gardens.

Pam Tait | Costume Designer

Theatre include *Top Girls* (Royal Court Theatre) as well as touring work with Hull Truck, Monstrous Regiment, English STage Company and Great Easter Stage.

Television include *Queer As Folk, In a Land of Plenty, Sid and Nancy, Pascali's Island, Beautiful Thing.*

Dance and cabaret include *Baller of Nations* (Impermanence Dance Theatre) and work for Thick and Tight Dance, Screaming Alley Cabaret, and English National Ballet.

Jess Tucker Boyd | Movement Director

Jess works as Movement Lecturer for the University West of London. Jess works as a freelance Movement Director, Director and Intimacy Coordinator. She is an alumni of East 15 Acting Schools Acting & Contemporary Theatre BA and The Royal Central School of Speech and Dramas MA in Movement Directing and Teaching.

Selected Movement Directing credits include: Shakespeare's Globe Theatre (*Hakawatis*), Royal Court Theatre (*Katzenmusik*),

Trafalgar Studios (*Coming Clean & BU21*), Bush Theatre (*Come Inside*), Theatre503 (*BU21*), Arcola Theatre (*Moormaid*), and Pleasance Theatre (*Honeybee*). Selected Intimacy Coordinator credits include: *Tattooist of Auschwitz* (Sky Atlantic), *BACON* (written by Sophie Swithenbank, directed by Matthew Illife), *One Day* (Drama Republic), *The Winter King* (Bad Wolf), *Dangerous Liaisons* (Playground productions), *I Hate Suzy* (Bad Wold/Sky Vision), *Missing Julie* (Theatre Clywd), *Faustus; That Damned Woman* (Lyric Hammersmith).

Rose Hockaday | Stage Manager

Rose Hockaday (she/her) is a Freelance Stage Manager based in London.

Theatre: *LORENZO* (2023 Fringe First winner), *Jali*, *Spellbound: Suhani Shah*, *Age is a Feeling* (2022 Fringe First winner and 2023 Olivier Award nominee), *Bedu* (Soho Theatre); *Worth* (New Earth); *Evita Too* (Sh!t Theatre); *harmony. 天人合一*, *At Broken Bridge*, *No Particular Order* (Ellandar); *The Ex-Boyfriend Yard Sale* (London & Toronto); *A Woman Walks into a Bank*, *Milk & Gall*, *Spiderfly*, *Wolfie*, *Art of Gaman* (Theatre503); *Antigone*, *Pops*, *You Only Live Forever*, *In Tents and Purposes* (Viscera Theatre); *Timmy*, *Glitter Punch*, *How to Survive a Post-Truth Apocalypse*, *They Built It. No One Came*, *Jericho Creek* (Fledgling Theatre).

Film: *Heaven Knows, Visitors, Ignite, Pomegranate, Wandering Eyes, Versions of Us*. As well as music videos 'Phase Me Out', 'When You're Gone', and 'Saint' for artist VÉRITÉ.

Eleanor Wright | Jean (VO)

Eleanor Wright is a professional actor and voice artist, and has toured with Toucan Theatre (*The Naughty Fox*) multiple times. Most recently she has worked with endorph_u productions on their latest short thrillers. Eleanor trained at Fourth Monkey, and as well as acting has worked extensively making theatre with young people in her community.

Hannah Farley-Hills for HFH Productions | Producer

HFH Productions is an award winning production company run by UK-based indie Theatre Producer, Hannah Farley-Hills. The company develops, mounts and tours theatrical productions nationally and internationally across both the subsidised and commercial sectors, showcasing drama and new writing that is bold, actively challenging and memorable. Hannah is passionate about collaboration that champions underrepresented perspectives and untested ideas. She believes a good play leaves you with more questions than it answers, things you should still be questioning in a week, a month, a year.

Over the last 10 years, Hannah Farley-Hills has worked on just shy of 35 professional productions both for organisations and independently, including Bacon by Sophie Swithinbank which transferred to Soho Playhouse in New York in January 2024. In 2023, Hannah was Associate Producer to international production company, Glynis Henderson Productions, working on Fix + Foxy's *Dark Noon*. Prior to that, Hannah was Associate Producer to London new writing company, Arch 468, and an in house Producer at leading regional venue, The Marlowe, where she developed and ran the Hope Prize Writer Commission and Roar new writing programme. Hannah is also currently Executive Producer of early years and disability specialist theatre company, Toucan Theatre.

Hannah received the Stage One Bursary in October 2020 and is an MGCfutures Bursary recipient. Hannah is a member of the League of Independent Producers.

SURRENDER

Sophie Swithinbank

in creative partnership with Phoebe Ladenburg

Foreword

For Phoebe, the first few years of motherhood were extremely challenging. Her now vibrant and hilarious daughter did not appear to enjoy being a baby and made it known, loud and clear.

During this time, while Phoebe was auditioning candidates for a London drama school, an applicant performed Kate's final monologue from *The Taming of the Shrew*. She had seen this oft-contested monologue performed many times, in many ways; eye-rolling, ironic, under duress, sarcastic. But this person performed it straight, believing every word; a version in which, fully indoctrinated, Kate has found peace in surrendering to the patriarchy. Phoebe recognised a parity with motherhood: it becomes infinitely easier if you just surrender to what is required of you. So Phoebe stopped fighting for independence, for agency, for her former self. Life did become easier, but departing from herself took its toll. The play sits on the knotty question of whether the expectations of motherhood and a belief in feminist values can coexist, even today.

Long-time friends and collaborators, Phoebe approached Sophie, asking her to write this story. After long conversations delving into all elements of Phoebe's experience, Sophie crafted a version of Phoebe's story, which explores Kate's journey of submission in *The Taming of the Shrew*, not through the lens of marriage, but through the lens of motherhood. First, Sophie wrote a poem in iambic pentameter, inspired by Kate's monologue. Then, slowly, over several years and many more hours of conversation, 'Mother' emerged as a fictitious character. When Phoebe started working with prison leavers, Sophie began to weave this into the story too. How does a woman and a mother fare, once she is 'in the system'? Mother is a woman who quietly, unwittingly, slips into a cascade of intervention, judgement and mistrust. She shows us just how easy it is to let things fall apart.

We know that this play is tangled with thorny and slanted ideas about feminism and motherhood. We look forward to people disagreeing with Mother, so that we can start an authentic conversation about exactly what happens when women become mothers, and what happens when mothers slip into crisis.

Phoebe Ladenburg and Sophie Swithinbank

Character

MOTHER, *thirty-nine*

(*Some scenes take place eleven years earlier.*)

Note on the Text

(/) indicates an interruption.

(,) indicates a beat.

(Words in brackets) are implied not spoken.

Note on Sound

Between each scene there is a sound, like a bone popping out of joint.

This text went to press before the end of rehearsals and so may differ slightly from the play as performed.

Visit

MOTHER (*thirty-nine*) *is in prison. Daughter* (*twelve*) *has come to visit.*

Daughter takes a seat. They are familial in their apperances.
MOTHER *looks at her Daughter; tears swell at her eyes, but she forces them away.*

MOTHER. We haven't even said hello yet and god look at me, I'm already…

They both laugh, a sense of relief.

Sorry sorry sorry. You're just so. You're just so incredibly beautiful.

Sorry. Is that…? / Am I being embarrassing?

Laughing.

Sorry.

I love your… style though. You have… does everyone wear stuff like this now?

Wow. Brilliant. With your own money?

Who gives you pocket money?

Mum. Yes. Course she does. That's… good. That's great! Really good.

Nothing else to say for a moment.

Great earrings. When did you get them piecered?

I miss wearing my jewellery.

Hey, I should… you should have it.

No I'm serious! I'll figure out a way to get it to you.

No. No. I'd really, really… why don't I send it? What's your address?

She has overstepped the mark here.

Sorry. No. I um… it's okay, you don't have to…

MOTHER *panics, has she messed it up already?*

I've actually been writing you letters for years. There's a library here… we get twenty minutes a week and I just go in there, smell the books, write to you. They don't tell me your address, I just write them and they post them so I don't know if they ever…

Oh you did get them?

That's. Okay that's great. I no, I wasn't expecting a reply.

,

We only have an hour. Well not even, actually. (*Little nervous laugh.*)

Do you think, do you think you'll stay for the whole time, or will you, do you want to leave earlier than / that's okay, if you do. I know it's – (*Gesturing to the horrible room.*) / sorry…

Oh. She picking you up at three? Okay good. That's perfect. Sorry. I just I have lot to say, and I'm sure you do too, and it might take me a while to get my, my thoughts in order, sorry.

She laughs.

Well, yeah, sorry, maybe I do say sorry a lot. Maybe because I know I owe you. I owe you endless debts, darling, I can't /

She can't finish the thought so she changes the direction.

You look like me.

You do. We've got the same… (*Vaguely gestures to her jawline.*) well. I think we do. But really, you barely know me.

Well, yes I know you know *about* me. That's not the same.

Well. I know you. Feels like I do. I mean, I knew you. I just, to be honest, with a mother like me, I don't know how you became so amazing.

She laughs.

Amazing all along? Darling, you were not amazing all along. (*Sotto.*) Not in the slightest.

Look, I don't know what version of events you've been told but…
this is the version I'd like you to hear, and then you can do
whatever you want, you can make up your own mind, okay?
You're a grown-up girl. This isn't, I'm not going to pressure you…

(*Direct address.*) And you. All of you,
It may be too late for me but it's not for you,
It's not too late for you.

So, soften, listen, soften, listen… Go.

Beginning

Eleven years earlier. Interrogation room, police station.

SFX: The Police Officer starts the recording, stating the date and time, but his voice is muffled and distorted. We can't make out the words, only that it is a male voice.

She paces, manic.

Yes, officer, okay. There was a time when I left her. To go out and meet a friend. But I left her with a… neighbour… a nice neighbour who had a nice dog. So the flat is all quiet and still like it's holding its breath so I hold my breath too, and I head out.

The Officer tells her to stop pacing and sit down.

Right. Yes. Sorry. Just…

She sits down.

I arrive at the café a little late but still, it's nice, just two women with no children, having a coffee, uninterrupted, you know? Well you don't know actually. Because you are man. They're precious, these moments are precious.

But the thing is, when I get there, something is wrong. My friend tells me I look shattered and I am I am single-parenting. I am doing this completely alone. Let's just, just bear that in mind, dear listener, if you will.

And I tell her I tried. I tried to be /

'*What do you mean "tried",*' she says, '*You're a wonderful mother. You're the best.*'

And I say, please don't look like that at me.
And she is moving, leaning closer
But it feels like she is moving further away.
And I say, don't.

LX: A sheet of glass seperates her from the audience.

(*Direct address.*) Because that scowl, you teach, that crumpled frown, frowning rage hot water, bubbling up from the centre of the earth and she's touching her face, or touching mine, and I feel this impact this heat, but only for a moment and then there's this glass, separating us. Like when you go to a museum and you see things but you're not allowed to touch them and it feels like you haven't really seen them at all.

(*To Daughter.*) You know that feeling, darling, don't you? You've been to museums? And, well, even though there's this glass… bubbles in the glass where the plastic coating has come away and I can't quite see…

SFX: The Police Officer speaks, dragging her attention back to the interview room.

LX: The sheet of glass dissolves.

The beginning? Right. No. Sure sure sure. It's hard to say what the beginning is, officer. Because the beginning could be when I got pregnant that was the official beginning of something changing, something changing and controlling and also the beginning could be when I went into labour or when she was born or when I… when I…

well no, I guess that's, that's actually sort of the end.

SFX: Very distant sound of a dog barking.

Water

SFX: The recording continues.

No I never hurt her. Not directly.

No I didn't drop her. I fell, holding her. I fell, but she wasn't injured, at all. I / broke my

Really? That seems a bit archaic.

Give me a polygraph then. Give me a
Polygraph then. Give it to me go on
give me a polygraph fucking give me /

She is given a cup of water and told to calm down.

No – Not – I am calm.

I don't need water, I'm not a plant.

,

I'd like a lemonade please.

Polygraph

She is wired up to the polygraph machine.

SFX: We hear the mechanic sounds of the machine, but not the questions.

Yes, I intend to tell the truth

London.

Twenty-seven.

She's sixteen months.

No.

No. Never.

No. Okay well maybe I've nicked a few things but nothing serious.

No, he's… he's not around.

I don't know. I don't know where she is. That's why I'm here.

Two days.

Tuesday. Morning.

Sorry no, I meant Wednesday. I thought today was Thursday.

No.

No. I just said that.

Security

She is alone in the room with a Security Guard.

Excuse me? Sorry, hi?
Have you got a vape?
Helloo.
I know you do, I saw you vaping outside.
I know you can hear me, you have ears.

(*Sotto.*) Rather large ones in fact full of baggy holes.
Sorry, I didn't mean to… sometimes I just say stupid…

Do you have to take all your piercings out when you come to work?

I bet they look great when they're in.

I bet you look totally different in your normal clothes.

I had to take out my belly bar when I got pregnant. But I made up for it by getting a nose piercing, which… didn't really work out in the end.

He gives her a vape.

Oh you star, thanks.

She gets up. He follows.

Why you following me?

I don't like being watched.

Well fine, watch me. But could you stand a little further away?

I can smell your sweat from here.

She vapes, he watches.

Whole Truth

In a better mood now, having vaped.

The thing with lies, right, is that they are invisible,
Lies are invisible, lies are the things that aren't there.
Nobody told me, for instance, what it would really be.
I have a small keeper of my body
I have a tiny keeper of my heart
And nobody told me about that.

So I know what lies are,
And I know what truth is
and this is the whole truth, okay?

So, listen, officer.
I had an audition for the *Shrew*.
I had arranged for my mother-in-law to

I had made arrangements, okay.
Like any other mother.

(*Carefully.*) I had made arrangements.

She cannot remember what the arrangements were.

Trial

(*Distracted.*) On Netflix there's this stupid film called *Bad Moms*. As if it's not hard enough already. So I throw my phone at the TV and it smashes and then I'm angry because the phone was expensive and I'm behaving like a baby and then my actual baby wakes up and starts her night-time screaming routine and I join in.

There's a unique type of, emptiness, when you're awake in the night and the rest of the world is asleep. Like you're the only one, blind almost, with hot eyes in the dark.

Do you know what I mean?

Do you have children?

(*Sotto.*) No. I thought not. You know, when you become a mum, there are all sorts of people who suddenly pass judgement over you, right from the very beginning. From how you behave during your labour, the last-minute epidural, labelled weak, from the very beginning, and then, how you hold the baby, how you breastfeed, or don't... and once you're flagged, once you're 'not coping', well it's a misogynistic pile of bullshit to be totally honest. And you. You should not be the person to pass this judgement, if you do not have children.

No, you are clearly qualified, but not for this.

I want an officer who is a woman. And a mother.

(*Sotto.*) Unsurprising.

I said. That's unsurprising. The officers who are mothers are probably all *at home*. Their careers, their careers...

You know, my agent dropped me when she was six weeks old. It's true!

Because I couldn't get to a a a... for some fucking commercial, because I couldn't leave the flat... (*Painful.*) because I was a different shape, my stomach, my body... unrecognisable – and you have to understand that as an actress /

Well no I wasn't claiming benefits, I had my office job.

Look. It's been forty-eight hours of this and I'm losing my fucking... (*Attempting calm.*) the time you're taking interrogating me is time you're wasting not looking for my baby. So what are your real priorities here? That's what I'd like to know. Because this feels more like a a a... a trial. Like you're testing me.

Audition

So. The day of the audition. In the casting call they said to bring a coat and I brought my favorite coat – (*Somehow has this prop with her.*) which always made me feel like an incognito celebrity, but – get this – when I got into the audition room the woman said, '*hard to dig out a coat at this time of year isn't it?*' and I said, pardon? and she said, '*is that something you've borrowed?*' and I said no. And she said, '*Oh! It does nothing for you, love. Here, pop this on.*'

Can you believe it? 'Pop this on.' The people in these places. If you're searching for a villain in this story, it's her. Or you actually. You're just recording people revealing their darkest memories, but you don't actually do anything to help.

It's not 'collecting evidence' if there's no crime.

I'm not saying you're bad at your job, I'm just saying your job is bad. The system doesn't work.

,

Anyway, the audition. I deliver my… I, my, fie

LX: She is now an actress.

> fie, unknit that threat'ning, unkind brow,
> And dart not scornful glances form those eyes.
> A woman moved is like a fountain troubled,
> Muddy, ill-seeming, thick, bereft of beauty.
> Thy husband is thy Lord, thy life, thy keeper…

… thy keeper, my little keeper…

'*I'm not quite, I don't quite believe you,*' the casting woman says. '*Try it again, and really believe it.*'

So I do it again, obedient, again and again but I can't quite find the…

She looks to Daughter. Smiles. Pushes on.

And then, on my way home I realised I'd left my nice coat at the audition. I'd accidentally left with the horrible coat the casting woman had lent me. So I nipped back.

I just nipped back. It wasn't far. But when I got there, they must have all gone home, because the building was closed. So my nice coat was lost and I was upset.

Woke

Sorry, quickly, off the record, I'm um, I'm sorry, okay, if
I offended you with what I said. You obviously are. Completely
qualified, and good at your job. It's actually a job / it's a really
impressive job. I just, I'd just like to be clear. So that you
understand really what happened… because I / she didn't sleep
for more than thirty minutes at a time, for the first three, four
months. And I'll just explain because, you've not had your own
experience of this, but a lack of sleep as severe as that, it becomes
an illness, it can lead to /

(*To Daughter, sharp and direct.*) Yes it is. It is an illness, darling.

And I. And things happened. And all I know is that I woke and
drifted and woke and drifted and woke into a completely different
version of myself.

And then when I really woke up – I'm not even sure I was ever
asleep to be honest, because I was fully dressed – but when
I really woke up

she wasn't there.

Lunch

MOTHER *is alone in the interrogation room. She has been given a sandwich, an apple and a can of Coke.*

She picks up the sandwich. Looks at the ingredients on the back. Puts it back down.

She is bored, restless, not hungry.

She stretches.

And then suddenly, she's upside down, in a handstand against the wall.

SFX: The metal door clicks open.

The Security Guard comes in.

(*Re the handstand.*) I just have to do this sometimes. When I've been sitting down too long.

No no, fine thanks.

The Security Guard leaves.

SFX: Metal door closes.

She remains in the handstand for a moment longer. Then comes down.

Right.

She picks up the apple and takes a bite.

That's actually quite a good one. Crunchy.

She enjoys the rest of the apple and it's suddenly very hard to feel mistrustful of her.

(*To Daughter.*) Do you remember, darling, you used to love cherries? Red cherry juice all over your face like a little vampire.

In here? Oh it's very basic really. Pasta with red sauce… pasta with green sauce…

The dessert is always yogurt which reminds me of you.

The others?

As if the others might be listening:

Oh, you know, they're okay. It's all women, obviously.

I just keep my head down.

Most of them um… theft, drugs… fraud.

No. No friends, really. People are very… if your crime involves a child… people are very… yeah, no friends really.

Actually, actually… there is one woman, Kate. From my wing. She's been through some… she's the one who actually suggested I invite you to visit. And at first I was like no way, because – (*Sotto.*) she's a bit nuts, Kate. But she kept saying it… that I owe you some kind of…

So I did it. It was terrifying, writing it and sending it, with the visit-booking form and the the rules, and you have to remain seated and… I felt so embarrassed, darling. For you to see me here.

But I did it. And I'm so glad I did. Because. Seeing you… this is the happiest I've been in…

Green Paper

MOTHER*'s hands, unconsciously, are in prayer.*

SFX: The recording clicks on.

Officer, I assume you are familiar with the Green Paper system?

Her hands break apart.

Jesus, the different departments really need to communicate. It's your own time you're wasting.

Well I'll just explain then, so that everyone's up to speed. What happened is that I, me, we two, my home, got flagged in the system, a Green Paper was issued that logs a 'concern about a child's safety and welfare'. And once you are a flagged on a Green Paper, you are assigned a visit from a social worker. So theoretically, a great system for the protection of children.

But. I was nervous about it. Nervous about the visit. Well, you would be, wouldn't you? Someone nosying about in your home, checking for mistakes. And if there are mistakes. The whole thing starts to feel like a bit of a witch-hunt, to be honest.

And I was, I couldn't sleep eat because, in the worst-case scenarios, they take the child away. But this. This was not a worst case scenario, okay?

(*To Daughter.*) Darling, you were fine, you loved… you loved cherries… and, and, and…

Eggs

SFX: A break from the recording.

Can I borrow your vape again? Last time, I swear.

Please. You're the only normal person here.

The Security Guard gives her one, it's easier than arguing.

Thank you. You're solid gold.

She vapes.

Just between you and me, Andreas, there was a time when I felt so train-wrecked, so completely hit by a brick wall, that I wondered if I was actually dead. I lay in the tangled covers and googled, 'can you die from...' and I was going to write 'a lack of sleep' but – get this right – it was the first thing that came up anyway. The first thing! I rolled off the bed and let the duvet fall off with me. I lay like that for quite a long time, a hidden lump inside the lump of duvet, heating up my cocoon with my own breath, wondering how long it would take to run out of oxygen.

And then I realised she was crying –

– and I wasn't sure how long she'd been crying for. I couldn't remember hearing her start crying, maybe maybe she had never stopped... and I got up, emerging from my airless chrysalis.

I made her scrambled eggs for breakfast that day. I made myself some coffee. Not a nice morning coffee with the papers and steam rising dustily through the morning sun. It was just petrol that would ensure I didn't just roll to a stop in the middle of the motorway.

I put the scambled eggs in front of her and straight away she knocked it onto the floor.

The memory hurts her.

I was starving, starved of free will,and I... and I fucking shouted and her mouth tightened and turned into a sad little rainbow for a second of silence before her whole face crumpled and she... but then she didn't. No titanic eruption. She was silent with this sad mouth, and I wondered why, and I realised she was scared. Of me. It was probably her first ever experience of fear.

And I cannot describe how awful. I cannot tell you what that feeling is. I don't think there's a word for it because nobody ever talks about it. This thing in parenting. Nobody talks about the very real possibility of becoming a bully.

I held her close to me and I trod the egg into the carpet, punishing myself and I said shhh shhhh I'm sorry.

Feeling suddenly overexposed, she shifts slightly away from the truth.

It was a windy day and one of the bedsheets on the balcony flew away but I didn't bother to get it and then some invisible thought made me check my phone and

The casting woman has offered me the job! A contract, a rehearsal schedule, a costume fitting.

And I can't be here, with her, with this egg on the floor,

so I go. I do go, yes. Because I am busy and I am successful.

(*Direct address.*) And I can see you're thinking now, you're thinking, we're getting there, we're getting to the good bit. Because you love this stuff, don't you? The documentaries… podcasts… true crime. It's a bit sick. It's a bit sick, really.

Unwinding to the notion that someone else's life is worse than your own. It's relaxing, in many ways, isn't it? Who's feeling relaxed?

LX: She shines a light into the audience, to see who is feeling relaxed.

Someone's stomach makes a noise.

Oh. Are you hungry?

I just heard your stomach making a noise.

Are you? Hungry?

No?

Well, let's stop wasting time, shall we.

LX: She turns off the light.

Dream

LX: Into the dark.

(*To Daughter.*) Do you ever have nightmares, darling? Do you ever write them down? In my letters to you, I often wrote about my dreams, didn't I? Did you (read them)? I have this one where I'm walking in the night, just walking in the calm, and I stumble over a pile of women who have no dreams at all.

LX: The light comes up over the following.

I can see, behind their eyes they have no thoughts at all, blank monsters, sucking me in and I do that thing in a dream where you try to run but you're completely stuck.

I call it a straitjacket dream, when you're stuck like that. It's sleep paralysis but you're not fully asleep… I was never fully asleep back then and it's it's it's exhausting…

(*To Security Guard.*) Hey, sorry, is it Andreas? Do you think I could just, get some sleep? I think I'm…

Yeah, I think that would really help.

Thanks.

In a cell, she is given a bedsheet and a pillow and she sleeps, with this song stuck in her head: 'Something's Happening' by Herman's Hermits.

Reality

Stuck somewhere between dream and reality.

SFX: The song continues, combined with distorted memories of the interrogation questions.

I have this job, on the side of my acting jobs. The side job is at an office where fairly important things happen and I have a fairly important role.

I cling to Outlook and clients and contracts and fees and Reply All and I attach the PDF. But I shout accidentally at an intern and I lose my staples and my stapler is empty. So nothing is stapled and everything falls apart. And at some point my line manager asks me if I'm getting enough sleep and I laugh, I honk loudly in his face. No, Richard. I haven't slept for three months. Now bring me some fucking staples.

Unconsciously, over the following, she gathers the bedsheet in her arms, holding it like a baby.

He brings me the staples and a coffee and I carry on for a while. But I'm not really real at work and I'm not really real at home. And I wonder if I'm really me at all. I howl in the toilet to see if I know my own voice, and I don't. I hurt myself, little tricks and cuts, to see if I know my own body, and, no, I don't.

Then at some point later, Richard asks me to go home, and when I get home I realise that he almost certainly doesn't want me to return. Why would he? So I call him and say, would you like me to quit, Richard, so that you don't have to carry the guilt of firing me right after my maternity leave? And he says… '*um er well no um it's just well*'… and I say I'm handing in my notice Richard. And he says, '*Right okay yes. Well.*'

She lets the bedsheet unravel.

And now the job is gone. No more staples.

I check my phone and the contract and the rehearsal schedule and the costume fitting are

also gone.

She drops the bedsheet to the floor.

I open my wardrobe and my coat – my lovely trench coat – is still there, hanging silently and untouched and I realise there hadn't been an audition at all. I don't even have an agent.

Social Worker

I had developed a lot of anxiety around the event of the social worker's visit, I had got myself into a tight lemon twist about it. But luckily, I'm an actor, I knew what to do.

None of it was lies though darling, it was all real, it was all real love, it just had to look correct in the eyes of the beholder. There's all these *things* they look out for. So I had consciously planned to get out all your nicest toys and and and smile a lot, because I knew – back from the time when people used to compliment me – that I had an attractive smile.

So she arrives and my palms are sweating but, incredibly, you're sound asleep. And I think perfect, perfect. So it's just her and me, and I can be very charming when I need to be, and I look great, and I make her a cup of coffee. I answer all her questions, which I thought would be about me – my parenting style, my mental health – but actually they are all about you, darling. Because that's the thing, the thing is that they don't care about the mothers. They only look into the child of the adult who has been flagged. I am just the Green Paper.

But then she asks if she can see you.

And I say that I'd rather not wake you, if that's okay.

But she says she needs to see the two of us together, before she can sign us off.

So I go upstairs and I pick you up. You wake and I smile and kiss you but you erupt.

Your loudness against my silence.
My silence continues indefinitely, deaf to me.
And she watches as I try to soothe you but…

I can't. You won't stop, you're hysterical. Maybe you're teething, but you're not. And I try to feed you and I try to pick you up and put you down and I try to burp you and I try Calpol but none of it works and she's still here. And then she says

'Why don't I take her?'

And I look up and I think this cannot be happening and I will get
a knife and cut out your tongue so you never tell anyone that
I cannot soothe my own daughter.

Please don't take her away, I say, breaking my silence.

*'No, love, no, I just meant, why don't I hold her for a bit, you take
a little break. She's in a right old pickle isn't she.'*

I stand completely still with you in my arms and slowly slowly,
I hand you over, all the while terrified that she will just run out
the door, take you away…

But then what actually happens is far worse:

You stop crying. In this woman's arms. She rocks you so sweetly,
she has such an ample bosom. She sings, softly, and you look up
at her, flaming red cheeks calming down to pink. She's done this
before, it shows in the fold of her arms.

'I've got three boys,' she says.

I've got three boys. What a thing to say. I've done this three times
over. It was easy for me.

Please could you take us off the Green Paper, I say. There's
nothing wrong here.

She says she can't do that because she's a little worried about me.

But you haven't asked me a single question about myself. I'm
fine, but you haven't even asked. Then she asks if there's a dad
and I consider explaining that he's not around any more. He never
will be. But I don't want to bring that heaviness into the… it's all
too delicate already.

So I just shake my head no; 'no dad.'

She says she's going to arrange to come back another time and
for ages I thought it was your fault, darling, it was your fault, but
but no

(*Soft.*) you were only a baby, it wasn't your fault at all.

Welling up, changing the subject.

Coffee Break

In the interrogation room.

As if she has just woken up/come to:

Sorry, hi – Andreas?

Where's everyone gone?

Right. (*Rubbing sleep from her eyes.*) Well can I have a coffee too please?

He goes to get a coffee. She puts the blanket and pillow away.

He returns with the coffee.

Thanks.

You know, this would be even better with a vape /

No. Okay. Gottit. Don't push it.

Despite its burnt and disgusting nature, she drinks the coffee.

What's the worst thing you've ever seen?

And don't say me.

Don't be silly(!)

Like you must have seen people… people you're proper scared of? When they have to get extra security in?

I won't tell / anyone

SFX: Metal door opens.

(*Clears throat.*) Hello officers.

Stealing

So. The second visit from the social worker. The recall, if you will. I was less anxious this time, I was more... strategy-focused. I got it into my head, somehow, that just needed more stuff. To show off my... parenting. Toys, changing mats, bouncers, fleecy pram sleeping bag, organic nipple cream, rosewater face mask, special stretchy knickers. And, as you can imagine, I couldn't actually afford these things so I just started... stealing is very easy if you've had any actor training. You learn how to get people to notice you in a room so you also learn how to get people to not notice you.

And I got a bit addicted to it, shoplifting. (*Sotto.*) It was so easy.

But then yeah. I got caught. I was with you, darling – it was all for you all this stuff.

No, no I'm not blaming you, please. Sorry, I'm just saying I was with you, with a lot of stuff hidden in the buggy. And they took me to the police station, and I was so humiliated. And they made me call someone to come and get you and the only person I could think of was Jean. Your daddy's mother. From before. Do you remember her?

Christmas? You have Christmas with her?

What about your foster parents?

They're friends with her? Why the fuck are they friends?

Darling, Jean is not, Jean is not our friend.

Listen. Calling Jean that day, was the biggest fucking mistake I ever made she's a muddy lying cunt and I can't believe you spend fucking Christmas with her!?

Forget it. I'm not going to sit here while you defend Jean. (*Checking time.*) Are we nearly done?

No. No wait, don't go. Sorry. We've still got fifteen minutes. I just get... please stay. Fifteen minutes.

Because, darling, the accusation is on me now and once it's on it doesn't go away and sometimes I think that you could feel my stress because you knew me. You lived inside my body inside my stress, my failings, for nine months and then you just arrived in the world and you didn't like it. I never liked it, and then you didn't like it at all and now my ghosts are your ghosts too. I can see it. My ghosts are…

Interval

I'm just trying to explain, officer, that this incident wasn't an isolated egg in its own shell, you know? I keep looping back because I'm not sure, at what point… I don't remember making the actual decision to… leave her.

Yes. You already know I did, I did leave. I did leave her. I don't know where. But I'm trying to say that I was completely gaslighted. I didn't know I was doing it.

Premeditated? Premeditated makes it sound like she's dead. So let's not. Let's not bandy that around.

Hey – (*To tech box.*) why don't we take a break?

She would like to stop performing now.

(*Gesturing towards someone in the audience.*) I can see this guy's tired.

You've had a long day, you had to rush to get here, you just want to go home. You're tired.

I can see you're all tired of me.

(*To tech box.*) Hello-o?

No response.

Fine. Well.

(*To Officer.*) I know you already know, officer, you just need a confession on the record, don't you? Because you don't have 'sufficient evidence'. I know how this works, I've seen… films.

Please stop saying you are trying to help me. No one is trying to help me, no one has ever helped me and no one ever will. He left me and now you will too. You all will. Sitting there, accusing me of neglect but when I needed help, no one was there and now, now it's too late.

Wait. What? Where are you going?

What's going on? Tell me.

She paces, frustrated.

SFX: A radio bleeps and crackles, commotion.
,
They've found her?

They've found her?!

Dogs

(*To Daughter.*) No, essentially, darling, I thought you were lost but I'd walked myself into a trap.

The neighbour found you. Well, the neighbour's dog actually. Muddy and…

A silence while they both consider the darkness of this.

If it hadn't been for that dog you might have died. That's what the papers said. They did a whole thing about the 'hero dog' and there was this horrible picture of me in the tabloids… and the judgement was heavy like tar, tarnish and rust.

Because I had been in a play, before I got pregnant and the reviews had been incredibly positive so people had sort of. Heard of me.

My agent saved all those reviews if you ever wanted to…. No. Sorry. Getting distracted!

She attempts to refocus…

Although one review said I was… 'on fire'.

Is Daughter impressed? Not really.

Sorry. Sorry. The point is, darling, journalists, you know, they love a scoop, a splash, a public fall from grace. So they made a huge deal of this… dog situation.

You know. I've often wondered whether you have an affinity with dogs. Are you one of those kids who strokes every dog?

Yes, she is.

I thought so. I had a feeling.

Oh really? Oh he sounds gorgeous. What's his name?

Banjo! Got any pictures?

Daughter has loads of pictures.

Oh he's lovely. So fluffy! Do you walk him every day?

I bet he adores you.

And you love him, don't you?

I can tell. He's lovely darling.

In-law

A recorded legal statement begins to play – JEAN *(voice-over).*

LX: A box slowly closes in around MOTHER.

JEAN *(voice-over).* On Wednesday the twenty-second of November the defendant left my granddaughter in the car for almost six hours –

MOTHER. No. I need a break. I need to use the bathroom.

LX: The box stops closing in.

(*Sotto.*) I'll just quickly tell you while we're in the toilet. So Jean (lying cunt) she moved in with us. After the time I got caught shoplifting. She moved in to Support Us. But what she was actually doing was Watching Me. Watching everything I did and building up this statement of things –

JEAN *(voice-over).* …in the car for almost six hours.

MOTHER. No.

JEAN *(voice-over).* In order not to alert passers-by, she had given my granddaughter a sedative to / make her sleep.

MOTHER. No, stop. What happened darling, what happened – (*Painful.*) is that she got custody of you.

JEAN *(voice-over).* She had gone into the shopping centre –

MOTHER. I don't know what version of events you've been told, darling, but *this* is the version. This is the real version.

JEAN *(voice-over).* From one shop alone, she stole nearly two thousand pounds' worth / of products –

MOTHER. Me. This. I was your mother. I still am.

JEAN *(voice-over).* On numerous occasions she left the house without planning childcare, and I'd have to rush home from work. She said that during these times she was 'sleepwalking' or 'living a different reality'.

MOTHER. All these little mistakes. These tricks and cuts.

JEAN (*voice-over*). Sometimes, during these 'episodes' she would take my granddaughter out with her, and I would receive these garbled text messages…

MOTHER. My job at the office is cancelled and I've found my coat in the wardrobe.

JEAN (*voice-over*). Whenever she did come home, the child screamed hysterically. I think she was scared. And honestly, I was scared of her too.

MOTHER. Well that's not. Real. Not not not. Factual. Darling, you were fine. You loved, you loved…

JEAN (*voice-over*). She tried to kill me.

LX: The box starts closing in again.

MOTHER *is scared and silent.*

She tried to poison me.

MOTHER*'s silence turns to laughter.*

MOTHER. This is ridiculous.

JEAN (*voice-over*). She planned it and plotted it.

MOTHER. She's mad. She's lying.

JEAN (*voice-over*). She mixed her medication in with mine.

MOTHER. That? That was a complete misunderstanding.

JEAN (*voice-over*). I had to go to A&E.

MOTHER. You, darling, you were sleeping and you were so beautiful, and I loved you so much and I knew in that moment that I didn't need anything else apart from you ever ever ever, and my heart hurt like it'd grown too big inside me. I picked you up and we went outside.

JEAN (*voice-over*). I am so glad my son had moved on before all of this.

MOTHER. You're glad, Jean? What's wrong with you?

JEAN (*voice-over*). It's not safe. Living with this woman.

MOTHER. What are you saying? He was the love of my life.

JEAN (*voice-over*). The love of your life?

MOTHER (*to Officer, a last-ditch attempt*). That's, that's another thing actually, that we've barely talked about. Because it's painful, but during that whole period of time I was grieving. My love. He was the love of my life was gone. I was doing this alone.

JEAN (*voice-over*). You were the one who –

MOTHER. No. Don't. He hadn't been well for years.

,

He took his own life, darling.

,

I'm sorry.

JEAN (*voice-over*). He couldn't bear it any longer.

MOTHER. I saw the joy in him, Jean. He had these sparks of joy that I alone could ignite.

He was wonderful, your dad.

,

(*To Jean.*) He came to visit me once. He brought me the nice soap, you know, the one we used to have?

JEAN (*voice-over*). What? When did he do that?

MOTHER. I can't… I don't know, time goes so funny in here.

JEAN (*voice-over*). He never did.

MOTHER. I miss him. Every day.

Just like I miss you, darling.

,

JUSTICE (*voice-over*). The defendant will be sentenced for neglect of a child under the age of fourteen years, theft of goods worth over four thousand pounds and planned attempt to kill or seriously injure. This sentencing code comes under schedule twenty-one. Minimum tariff eleven years, upper tariff fourteen years.

SFX: Gavel.

MOTHER. So yes I left you darling, but you never left my heart.

LX: The box opens out.

Keeper

Now, if you recall, I'm with this friend, in the café, and she thinks I should still be strong and still be a feminist, and be fighting for change, and loving lots of different men at once, and having opinions about films and buying a vibrator and doing whatever the fuck I want, but I can't do that. I can't do any of that.

So I tell my friend the truth and – I never should have told her to be honest – because she's the one who told me to go to the police. And that was a big mistake, because that's when we were separated, really separated, I mean. That was the final sheet of glass.

LX: The sheet of glass seperates her from the audience.

'*I know it hasn't been easy*,' she says, my friend.

And even the word 'easy' offends me, and bristles rising,
I have a small keeper of my body
I have a tiny keeper of my heart
…thy Lord, thy life, thy keeper…
My thoughts are not my own, or mostly so.

I thought there was this role to play but I
I had this longing in a dangerous nook
A quiet that I cherished for myself

'*But that's okay, she says, that's okay. We all do.*'

Do you? I don't think you do because
It's not okay, it never was okay.
Even all while she built her tiny nest,
Even all while bright skin uncrumpled, stretched
Reached out soft arms, and drew first dewy breath
Did I keep little keeper in the dark.

The sleepless dark, I say, the constant light
All in a semi-bright and waking dream
I was not needed there, I see that now –
She was her own and I awake alone.

Yet craving nothing nothing at all but me,
Her sea-salt wet face, her salt-lick cheeks red.

I watched sometimes with unbelieving stare
I watched sometimes, she cried, I left her there.

I know. I owe her everything I have
I know I owe her endless debts of soul
But with sharp lemon twist I kept my nook
Because you.

'*Me?*' she says, '*Me?*'

You. With your fist raised and your third wave
Rolling forwards, towards shores, unshifting sand.
But the waves just hung there stuck with no swell –
It was not as you said, we could not rebel.

So walking in the night, just walking in the
Calm, I stumbled tripped fell over a pile of
Women. These women had no dreams at all
And tired from the journey, tired now
I lay down softly and I joined their lull,
I lay down my sword and I alone found…

My friend repeats and repeats my quiet name
which bouncing bounces empty off me,
and her hand strikes hot against my face
and she asks the sad question again

'*Where is she?*'

and I don't know and I don't know and I don't know.

Nobody told me.
Nobody told me I would have no body
Hands beneath her feet, I was bound to kneel
Before the tiny fists of fighting love.

SFX / LX: A buzzer goes. The sheet of glass dissolves.

It's the end of the visiting session. Daughter gets up to leave.

Have you / was this nice? Will you visit again?

Right. No, of course darling.

You know, when I get out, the custody can be reviewed.

Might you um, will you want to try again maybe? With me?

But, will you think about it?

Okay. I um, we're allowed to embrace. At the end. We're allowed to hug. If you…

They embrace, it's like coming home, MOTHER *cries.*

Okay darling, I, um, I love you.

Daughter leaves.

SFX: The door closes, metallic and hard.

(*Direct address.*) So I let her go.
I forfeit the right to raise life from seed,
I lose the warmth of her skin against mine.
And I know you're thinking, this won't happen to me.
But it's so easy, to let it all fall
It's so easy, sign the Green Paper
It's so easy. *I've got three boys. I've done this three times over.*
And even the word 'easy' offends me, and bristles rising and no…

…remember bristles falling
And wind falling
And fist falling from the sky
And gaze falling to her eyes.
It's not easy, but please, hear me,
cause it's too late for me but not for you.

So file, bend, smooth rough edges to survive:
get busy tending mending in the hive
Shrews yes, but tamed still.
Shrews yes but stand still,
Stand transformed, in motherhood
Melt transformed and find you are…

Soft. As a bear, a plaything,
Wide ocean eyes searching, look through,
Searchlight bright eyes seeking only you
Her light burrows into your heart headlong
And you must rest, and see where you belong.

So come now – soften, come surrender here,
And let yourself be small and needed near.
Our spirit our old nook, makes space for nest
Just let the ocean light inside to rest.

…Unknit that threat'ning, unkind brow…
Let kite strings cutting sky fall all around
Let the wind drop, let the kite fall
Let hips dance and sway and bounce your keeper.

Arms open heart open hands open wide
Find sweet comfort here, let your white flag rise.

End.

Acknowledgements

With thanks to Bristol Old Vic, Kate Burdette, Andrew Fingret, Rhy Hanbury-Aggs, Charlie Partridge, Kit Proudfoot, Bibi & Steve Rainey, Sara & Alex Ratcliffe, Jan Ryan, Kristin van Santen, Jocelyn Warwick-Ladenburg, Joseph Warwick-Ladenburg and Caroline Warwick.

A Nick Hern Book

Surrender first published in Great Britain as a paperback original in 2024 by Nick Hern Books Limited, The Glasshouse, 49a Goldhawk Road, London W12 8QP, in association with HFH Productions

Surrender copyright © 2024 Sophie Swithinbank with Phoebe Ladenburg

Sophie Swithinbank and Phoebe Ladenburg have asserted their right to be identified as the authors of this work

Cover photography & design by Alan Harford @thestablelondon

Designed and typeset by Nick Hern Books, London
Printed in Great Britain by Mimeo Ltd, Huntingdon, Cambridgeshire PE29 6XX

A CIP catalogue record for this book is available from the British Library

ISBN 978 1 83904 372 7

CAUTION All rights whatsoever in this play are strictly reserved. Requests to reproduce the text in whole or in part should be addressed to the publisher.

Amateur Performing Rights Applications for performance, including readings and excerpts, by amateurs in the English language should be addressed to the Performing Rights Manager, Nick Hern Books, The Glasshouse, 49a Goldhawk Road, London W12 8QP, *tel* +44 (0)20 8749 4953, *email* rights@nickhernbooks.co.uk, except as follows:

Australia: ORiGiN Theatrical, *tel* +61 (2) 8514 5201,
email enquiries@originmusic.com.au, *web* www.origintheatrical.com.au

New Zealand: Play Bureau, 20 Rua Street, Mangapapa, Gisborne 4010, *tel* +64 21 258 3998, *email* info@playbureau.com

USA and Canada: Curtis Brown Ltd, see details below.

Professional Performing Rights Application for performance by professionals in any medium and in any language throughout the world should be addressed to Curtis Brown Ltd, Cunard House, 15 Regent Street, London, SW1Y 4LR, *tel* +44 (0)20 7393 4400, *fax* +44 (0)20 7393 4401, *email* cb@curtisbrown.co.uk

No performance of any kind may be given unless a licence has been obtained. Applications should be made before rehearsals begin. Publication of this play does not necessarily indicate its availability for amateur performance.

www.nickhernbooks.co.uk/environmental-policy

www.nickhernbooks.co.uk

facebook.com/nickhernbooks

twitter.com/nickhernbooks